To David

Best Wishes.

Jim Gaspari

CONFESSIONS
OF AN ARCHITECT

James S. Gaspari A.I.A.

authorHOUSE®

AuthorHouse™
1663 Liberty Drive, Suite 200
Bloomington, IN 47403
www.authorhouse.com
Phone: 1-800-839-8640

First published by AuthorHouse   3/24/2008
ISBN: 978-1-4343-6394-7 (sc)

Printed in the United States of America
Bloomington, Indiana

This book is printed on acid-free paper.

This book is dedicated to all the Architectural students and interns who never were taught, during their architectural education, of the situations they may experience when they become licensed and have clients of their own.

Contents

PREFACE:

We must all remember that one life's incident, no matter how insignificant it seems at the time, may be a turning or starting point in one's life. When I was a sophomore in high school, I was given an assignment in English Class to research and write a term paper on the profession of Architecture.

I had known of the profession but never gave it much thought. I did my research, spent time in the Public Library and enjoyed the research. I found out that Architects were artists with materialistic skills and were creators of living and working spaces.

I discovered that since I was picked out by my teachers to do artwork in the classroom and had no problem with the math courses I possessed some of the traits mentioned in my research. As far as the creative ability goes I learned from my mother that I was creative.

I was given an erector set for my birthday. It had lots of pieces and bolts and nuts and came with directions and illustrations of things to make by bolting the pieces together.

I didn't follow any of the directions but made my own objects as I saw fit. This bothered my mother who felt I had some disability not being able to follow the directions or illustrations.

1

When I wrote my term paper I discovered that I wasn't disabled but only creative.

I received a good grade on my paper and from that time on I wanted to be an architect. The important lesson I learned is that if one can establish his or her direction in life at a young age, it is easy to accomplish the goal by concentration of the direction and not being distracted by other influences which may be detrimental to the progress. I feel that it is important for parents to view the skills of their children and expose them to fields of endeavor which suit their skills. The child will make the decision of which field to enter but it will most likely be the field which involves the natural ability. What comes easy is what one should follow in life because it will be the most joyful.

Along the way I learned other lessons which are important in any field or profession. I learned the difference between sight and visions, hearing and listening and reading and understanding. To fully understand the problem is the key to finding the solution.

In the middle of my career, I was appointed to the State Board of Architects. This is the body that controls the practice of the profession and examines candidates for licensure. We were concerned with Life, Safety and Welfare.

One of my assignments was to help compose the questions on the written examination. There was a lot of technical stuff regarding life Safety and Building Codes and how to calculate the size of structural members. But my favorite question was one in the Welfare category. "Why is it important for an Architect to study the History of Architecture"? The simple answer is that regardless of the era that buildings are designed they must always contain the same elements of building design which are the Social, Physical and Economical considerations.

The buildings which are built are the fossils of the society of the civilization which creates them. This is true now as it has been in the past. Today's Architects must follow the same steps; solve the same problems as Architects in the past. The building technology may change but the steps are the same. Some of the elements may overlap but they are all part of the whole.

Social: No building is ever designed or constructed if there is no need for it. The Social make-up of the civilization determines the need for the Architecture. This is true for the prehistoric civilizations as well as the Egyptian Pyramids, Round Amphitheaters, Gothic Churches and Contemporary Skyscrapers.

The physical considerations are the climate topography, life sustaining elements such as water, air quality and the presence of indigenous building materials such as wood, stone and more recently iron ore and cement.

The economic factors are the ability to sustain a work force and have indigenous materials in substantial amounts (also part of the physical elements), the availability of technicians who know how to build with the latest technology of the times and the availability and ability of the government or client to finance the project.

If we know and understand these three elements we can enjoy a successful practice.

For the past forty years I have been practicing Architecture in the State of New Jersey. During that time I focused my business on general practice meaning that, without a particular area of specialization, I would perform architectural services for any client who needed or wanted them. Consequently, my projects were carried from small to large and from private to public, to medical and religious and all types of industrial and residential. Averaging about seventy-five projects a year, I have performed architectural services for about three thousand clients.

As time went by I experienced many situations which were unexpected, and humorous. Without using any names I would relate these situations with my fellow architects, my wife and my social friends. Their comments always contained the message that I should record these incidents and write a book which would be great reading. I always prefaced my story telling with the phase: "This is really true because I do not have the ability to make-it-up". So here they are – the stories are true but the names are made up.

Before I could open my office I had to finish my education and internship. I also had to meet my military obligation.

1. AT WAR WITH THE ARMY (PART ONE):

I consider myself a very patriotic American but the title of this Chapter is intentionally ambiguous since my military experiences leave me in doubt as to who fought for whom.

I attended college right after the Korean War was supposed to be over. Like many of my fellow students I wanted to finish my education and eliminate the possibility of being drafted. Consequently I decided to join the R.O.T.C. Program.

I decided to join the Air Force R.O.T.C. because I wanted to avoid infantry combat and flying seemed to have a better future.

When I arrived to sign up the sergeant in charge said that I had to take an I.Q. exam for entrance into the program. No problem I thought. I had graduated first in the class in High School and my College Boards results (SAT) were quite good. I was accepted to all of the colleges to which I had applied.

"Where do I take the exam" I asked quite confident of my ability to do well. "In the Law Building at 1400 hours this afternoon" was the reply.

"Let's see" I thought, "minus 12 is 2, so the exam is at 2 P.M. in the Law Building. Ok, I'll be there".

One of my faults is that I'm always on time. While I assume this is a good trait, it does provide some stress in my life. To this my friends will attest.

At 1:55 PM, excuse me, at 1355 hours I arrive at the Law Building to take the exam. It was in the middle of September on a hot and humid day. I was wearing slacks and a short sleeve open shirt.

I was met at the door by a uniformed guard who refused me entrance to the building. "You can't go into the building without a jacket and tie, this is the Law Building" he said. I told him that I was required to take the Air Force Entrance Exam which was about to start in five minutes. I was already sweating because of the heat of the day and my anxiety of being on time. "Come back with a jacket and tie" he said and I did an about face and started for my dorm room which was about ten minutes away.

My mistake was to run back to get a tie and jacket and return for the exam. I should have missed the exam and requested a new exam. The exam was half over when I returned but since it was a multiple choice exam I answered all the questions in the time that was allotted. Obviously this was not the way to score well.

I never was told what my score was but I didn't get accepted into the Air Force R.O.T.C..

I ended up applying to the Army R.O.T.C. and was accepted with open arms. My guess was that they were used to getting the Air Force rejects.

Now another decision arose. Which branch of the Army R.O.T.C. would I select? My choices were: the Infantry, the Quarter Master or the Transportation Corps. My thought process was easy and quick.

I don't want the Infantry because that's what I was trying to avoid by joining the Air Force.

I don't want the Quartermaster because my University had one of the most famous business schools and all of these "business majors" would outshine me in the Quartermaster Corps.

Transportation was my only solution and I thought I would rather ride somewhere than walk. After a short interview by the Army Recruiter I was accepted because "I liked cars and trucks". I had no idea at the time that the Army Transportation Corps. ran railroads, ships and airplanes.

I did very well in the R.O.T.C. Transportation Corps. I enjoyed courses and I did learn about trucks, trains, ships and airplanes. In fact I did so well that in my senior year I was promoted to cadet colonel and was in command (hypothetically) of all the other cadets.

As glorious as this was it set-up the stage for another battle. During my time in college the war in Korea had ended and troops were being discharged and were coming home. There was no longer a draft and the R.O.T.C. commitment had been revised. The two year program which had been a requirement had been revised to allow an option to the graduate to serve only six months. This was good news to me as I wanted to start my Architectural Internship as soon as possible (Architectural Internship is a minimum of three years and after five years at college a reduction of eighteen months in the Army commitment would allow me to enter into practice while I was under thirty years old.

Naturally I wanted the six month program but I encountered another problem. As the cadet colonel and being in the top half of my graduating class I was in line to receive a DMG award. This is a Distinguished Military Graduate award and according to the Army Regulations it carries with it the same commission as a West Point Graduate and the same commitment of serving in the U.S. Army for two to four years. I was warned that to refuse to accept this commission would be an insult to the military and my six month option would be denied and I would probably have to spend two years in Korea with clean-up forces still stationed there.

What could I do? I was seventh in my graduating class of fourteen. (We started as seventy-five freshmen and five years later there were only fourteen left). Being a patriot as I am, I bit my lip and accepted my fate.

On the last day of R.O.T.C. the PMS & T (The Professor of Military Science and Tactics) called me into his office. I reported and saluted in the correct military posture. "I have bad news for you" he said. I didn't know what was coming. Maybe war broke out somewhere in some remote area far worse than Korea and I was scheduled to go there, I thought. He continued "We just learned that you will not be graduating in the top half of your class and you cannot be awarded a regular Army Commission. We here all know that you deserve it but we're not allowed to change the rules. I'm very sorry".

I fought to keep the smile off my face and wondered what happened to my class standing. I was dismissed; I saluted, and left the office heading to the Architectural School. The other seniors were consoling the student who was to graduate but failed his Thesis Project. He would have to take the last semester over.

Hey wait, this means that I am seventh in a graduating class of thirteen. That puts me in the second half of my class, hurray, I don't have to go to Korea for two years.

But the war with the Army continues. I did get an assignment to the Active Army Transportation Corps. for a six month tour of duty. I had gotten married directly after graduation and my wife and I moved to a garden apartment about ten miles from the Army Base. My wife was a good sport and decided to take some graduate courses in a near-by college while I did my six months.

I reported to the base, took my physical and was then interviewed by an officer in personnel. "What did you do in civilian life?" he asked. "I'm an intern architect" I replied. "Is that similar to engineering" he asked. "It's an allied field", I responded weakly. We architects do not like being referred to as engineers but I had no time or choice to make another answer.

"O.K." he said, "I'm assigning you to an Engineering Battalion here on post. "We don't have any architects".

He gave me the location of the Engineering Battalion and off I went. To my surprise my assignment wasn't to a "Construction" Engineering Battalion but a Railroad Operating Battalion. So much for the smarts of the Personnel Staff. What do architects know or do with railroads? But here I am.

I reported to the headquarters and when they found out that I was an architect they assigned me to the Railroad Construction Company. "Maybe I'll design a railroad station" I though naively.

The first sergeant greeted me and ushered me into the Officer's Day Room. There were about ten second lieutenants playing pinochle at two tables laughing and smoking and not really noticing me. I went up and introduced myself and some kind soul offered to teach me how to play the game "What do you do all day here", I asked. He answered smiling "This is it but sometimes we drive the Captains wife to the P.X. (Post Exchange) for shopping and carry her bags home. Other times we write Efficiency Reports for all of us as the Captain is almost illiterate and makes us do each others Efficiency Reports". He handed me a typed page which contained a list of adjectives which were intended to be used in the Reports. "We have to be careful not to use the same adjectives in the same sentences on different Reports" he continued. "The rest of the time we play golf or go swimming at the Officer's Club". I had to take this sitting down but there were only a few empty chairs.

The next day I requested to see the Company Commander Captain Bohunk. He saw the troubled look on my face and asked "what's the matter". "I need an assignment, Sir, I replied. I don't want to play cards all day".

He looked at me and smiled and said "you're an Architect? You may be in luck. Last weekend one of the wooden railroad trestles burned and it was difficult to put out the fire because of the creosote. The trestle is being replaced and I can assign you to the bridge and building platoon if you would like". "Yes, Sir" was my reply.

Overnight I became the leader of the Bridge and Building Platoon which consisted of forty enlisted men and a Master Sergeant in Control. (Platoon leaders are always Second Lieutenants with a Master Sergeant as second in command). I drove up to the site and got and returned a salute from the Sergeant. "At ease, I said, I'm here to learn and to help. I'll work with you and won't pull any military crap, O'K". He smiled and said "Yes, Sir".

We all had a good time. I learned how to operate a bulldozer and crane and handled all the paper work that the sergeant disliked. I also learned how to weld and was able to repair some equipment which was damaged during the demolition and repair of the trestle. The project was finished ahead of schedule.

The trestle job was good for me but the bad news was I was back in the Day Room learning pinochle.

The door to the room opened with a bang and the First Sergeant looked at me and said "Lieutenant, Sir, the Post Commander wants to see you immediately, the jeep is outside waiting".

I got into the vehicle not knowing why I was wanted or what I had done to be so hastily treated. We arrived at Post Headquarters, the Sergeant knocked on the door and ushered me in.

I did remember my military courtesy and entered the room, snapped to attention and saluted. "Sir, Lt. Gaspari reporting as ordered". He was a Brigadier General. I had never met a General before. Seated along side his desk was a full colonel who I later found out was the Battalion Commander. They returned my salute, smiled and the General said "relax Lieutenant. I have a top secret mission for you". I was stunned but smiled in return but still stood at attention.

He continued. "We were watching you during the repair of that railroad trestle and were very pleased with the result". (So that's what that helicopter was doing as each day we got a fly over). "I am assigning you with ten dump trucks, two cranes and two bulldozers and their crews and operators. Here are the drawings for the back nine of the Officers golf course. I want you to clear the trees and grade the course". Any questions? "Yes, Sir, why is this a top secret project? I don't have a Top

Secret Clearance". "The funds for this project are coming out of Insect Control. Good Luck".

I saluted, did an about face and left his office. "Wow, I am a patriot, I did my job, had a great time, the six months went fast and I received a Letter of Commendation at the end of my tour of duty. They wanted me to "re-up" but I had my internship to serve. I never played the course I built but I have heard that it is a good one, so the Army and I both won that war.

1A. At War With The Army (Part Two):

Since I knew that my tour in the Army would only be six months and because I wanted to intern for a large prestigious firm, I chose to look for a place to live and work in New York City.

My military obligation at that time for Six Months Lieutenants was a total commitment of eight years, six months active duty, seven and a half years active reserve which included two weeks a year at summer camp and once a week night meeting. I could accomplish both my military obligation and my internship simultaneously.

Good deal, when I was a kid my folks never sent me to summer camp so now I could make up for the short comings of my youth. The counselors would be older and so will my fellow campers but a paid vacation in the country seemed reasonable.

With the help of my family, my wife and I did get an apartment on the upper west side of Manhattan and I got an internship with one of the largest Architectural Firms in the country. They were located downtown on Park Avenue.

My next assignment was to find a U.S. Army Reserve Unit which was located nearby the office so I could attend my weekly meetings without having to commute in the City after work and then have to commute home again after the meeting.

I found a unit which was in walking distance to my office. I signed on. They were happy to take me in. What I didn't realize was that, this unit, so favorably located in downtown Manhattan was also as prestigious as the Architectural Firm for which I was working. There were two Generals, twenty-five full Colonels and about fifty Company Grade Officers who outranked me. Most of the enlisted men and non-commissioned officers were college graduates who were practicing lawyers, accountants, banking officers and large chain department store executives. My immediate commander was a Superintendent of Schools in a prestigious near-by city. Boy, were we prestigious. Now they could boast that they even had an architect on staff.

I learned early on that "prestigious" could be not such a good thing. After about two years in the unit, the unit was recalled into active status and we shipped out to the South for active duty. Obviously the government had an eye on us as such a prestigious unit and we got the call.

As I noted before, I am a patriot, so I packed up my pregnant wife and headed South to resume my military career. By this time I had the rank of First Lieutenant and my military occupational status (MOS) was that of a Transportation Logistical Officer. My job was to determine how many cars, trucks, trains, ships and airplanes would be needed to support a specific military operation any where in the world. I also had a top secret clearance so I can't divulge any of the details of my military work.

But moving to the South created situations worth mentioning. Because a lot of Reserve Units were recalled at the same time, finding housing for my wife and family was difficult. In the Army to acquire housing on the post to which you were assigned one had to qualify by date of rank. That means that the Generals get first choice, then the Colonels and so on down the pecking order. But each rank was classified by the date that the officer attained such a rank. As recently promoted First Lieutenant I was on the end of the line for housing for First Lieutenants. I tried to find housing off-post.

Some of the local civilians had no use for military men and if they wanted to rent apartments they had signs up reading "no dogs of service men". Some patriots they were.

I was offered a single room with a kitchen counter on one end with an adjoining bathroom. The space was large enough but it had a dirt floor. I couldn't believe it. I knew my marriage would be in trouble if I ever signed up for this space.

I did find a place that was occupied by a soldier who was on active duty but was sent overseas with his unit. This was a common occurrence. I found out because my unit was called up to replace active units that were signed overseas.

We lived in this house several months until post housing became available to us by date of rank. There were seventeen thousand reservists who replaced and augmented the Army Post population.

Not all things were bad. My immediate commander was a very good golfer and after each tiring session of Transportation Logistics, he ordered me to the Post Golf Course and actually taught me how to play. It was ironic, here I was the second time around in the Army and I'm involved with golf.

We never short changed our military responsibility for golf but I confess I let my wife down when she needed me. Our baby was due any day but my Commanding Officer (C.O.) decided that we had worked hard and deserved a visit to the golf course. Off we went and I told my wife if she needed me to call the Golf Club House and they would page me.

It was such a nice day that, after finishing eighteen holes, we decided to play another nine. We did and there was no paging from my wife. When I returned home, I found her on the floor doubled over. She could not get up to make the phone call. I carried her into my car and drove to the hospital. My son was born fifteen minutes later.

The army doctor came to see me after the delivery and asked "why did you wait so long"? My answer was a weak "I was following my C.O.'s orders". Fortunately he didn't ask any more questions as he may have thought that he didn't have security status or the "need to know" to ask any.

My wife forgave me as the delivery was quick, painless, we had a new healthy baby boy and the total cost was seven dollars.

Of course my in-laws came to visit as soon as my wife was released from the hospital and was impressed with the situation. I made the mistake of taking them to the Officer's Club for a roast beef dinner. This cost about two dollars and fifty cents per person and they were impressed with the quality of the meal and its cost. I didn't have my Architectural License yet and my mother-in-law suggested that it would be a good idea to stay in the Army since the living was good and expenses were low. I knew then that I would never allow her to see the inside of the P.X.

There were some memorable times during my second tour in the military. One was the briefing of the United States

Secretary of State. I helped plan the logistical transportation portion of an oncoming military operation. Our whole unit put a lot of time completing the report for his briefing. He thanked us and went back to Washington. Some time later I found out from reading the newspaper reports that our advice was not followed. I was saddened by the unnecessary loss of life of fellow Americans.

But there were other times when orders from the Pentagon evolved into humorous activities. A directive came to us from Washington that our unit had to do mandatory amphibious training.

This was actually impossible to comply with the directive as the camp we were located in was about two hundred miles to the nearest body of water which could support an amphibious operation. The General had an idea and consulted with my section to see if it would work.

Logistical Transportation Officers knew how to unload ships of cargo and soldiers in a combat situation. During an invasion, when men had to be transported from ship to shore by small craft landing vessels, a "save all net" would be cast off from the loading deck of the ship to the water below. The men would climb over the rail and make their way down the rope netting which, as a square mesh network had hand and foot holds at every foot of fabric in both directions.

The plan was simple. Our headquarters building, being situated in the South, had exterior corridors or balconies open to the weather. The balconies were protected with steel railings not much dissimilar from the railings at the sides of ocean going troop ships. We were to provide save-all-nets (a Transportation Corps Item) with enough length to reach the ground from the third floor balcony railing. With all our weapons, back packs and in military combat clothing we were required to go over the railing on the third floor and climb down to the ground.

When the rest of the post became aware of what our unit was going to do, they got the time schedule and proceeded to our building to witness the "amphibious event". We were required to make three descents – the final one at 0200 hours. We were all surprised to see the turnout of people which included the military, their wives and children, as well as our own families. The engineer's group provided us with spot-lights which made the seeing easy and several hundred of us did the climb.

The whole deal was accepted by the Pentagon and we accomplished our mission without any injuries. A few months after that amphibious incident the need for our services was terminated. We were all glad to go home but to this day I wondered if our amphibious solution had anything to do with our release from active duty.

1B. BREAKING EVEN WITH THE ARMY:

After being released from active service I continued completing my reserve obligation. At the same time I was able to continue my architectural internship.

When my internship was completed I applied to take the Architectural Registration Exam (ARE) for licensure into the profession. This had been my goal since high school. My application was accepted and I started to study. The exam consisted of seven parts;

Architectural Design, Site Planning, Structural, Mechanical and Electrical Equipment, Construction Methods, Architectural History and Professional Practice. They were given on four days of one week and in two different locations. One location was the Local Architectural School and the other in an Army National Guard Armory.

It was a grueling week both mentally and physically. The five hour Structural Exam and the three hour Construction Method Exam were given on the same day in the Armory. (The twelve hour Architectural Exam was given on the previous day at the Architectural School).

The Armory was a huge open space where the State determined that the Lawyers, Nurses, Physical Therapists and Dental Hygienists could all take their respective exams at the same time. The fact that some exams were only two hours long or three hours long or five hours along, didn't seem to be a concern of the State. They all started at the same time so that as each exam ended while others were still working the call for dropping pencils and collection of papers made quite a distraction in this big room where approximately one hundred and fifty people of all professions were trying to concentrate.

I finished the first exam and ate my brown bag lunch. The second exam of Construction Methods began on time and I was ready. I had looked at my notes during lunch.

The room was half empty as some of the other exams didn't require a second session. It started to rain and as luck would have it, the bridge table to which I was assigned was directly under a hole in the long span roof of the Armory. I moved my table out of the rain drops and dried off the few drops on my paper. "What's next", I thought. Taking the exam under these conditions was not mentioned in Architectural School.

There was a "next". About thirty minutes into the exam, a huge steel roll-up door started grinding and opening, clanging and banging all the way up. When it was fully opened, at least twelve feet high, a military tank revved up and rolled into the testing room. I guess they didn't want it to get wet. What about the exam takers? They shut it down but it remained in the room. I felt the Army was still after me.

The last question on the exam was to Sketch the Design of a Long Span Structural System. I hadn't studied this and was surprised at the question. Equally unaware must have been the exam writer's as the answer to the last question was looming right in front of me. The Long Span of the Armory was composed of three hinged arches, exactly the answer to the question. I immediately forgave all the disturbances, sketched what were in front of me and finished the exam. I passed and received my license.

2. Opening Office:

When I decided to open my office it was because I had been approached by a client who needed a large industrial building. He wanted me to visit a seventeen acre site that he was contemplating buying but needed assurance that it was suitable for his project.

Since I was starting a new practice and had a potentially large project, I needed to rent an office space immediately. I contacted a realtor and made an appointment to see an office space which was the right size for me, a secretary, and a draftsman.

I met the realtor at the space and while it was the right size for me, the rental cost was not acceptable to me as the realtor owned the building and wanted a three year lease with large escalation rental rates every year. I declined and walked out in a hurry. I found another office space that afternoon and signed a much more reasonably priced lease.

The next day I met my new client who drove me to his seventeen acre site. Waiting there was the realtor whose office building I had refused to rent the day before. My client told me that he was buying the land from this man and needed me to confirm that the site was suitable. When the realtor realized what my role was he turned pale and appeared to be ready to faint. He did confirm that he had known me but could say no more.

In the end I recommended that my client should buy the property because it was zoned properly and in a well established area with rail and truck access.

I never had another deal involving the realtor, although we met from time to time on social occasions. He always had a big smile for me and told everybody in earshot that I was such a wonderful architect and his great friend.

3. Needing Glasses:

The first week on my own in my own office I noticed that I was developing eye strain after I had completed some preliminary drawings. My new secretary, who was a part-timer, suggested that I see an Optometrist. She recommended a new guy in town who had just opened his own practice.

Without calling, I paid him a visit and found him behind an empty desk in a shabby waiting room. He was flipping through a phone book looking a little perplexed. I made a little cough to attract his attention but got no response. He kept looking and flipping through the pages.

I stood there awhile thinking that he is the one needing glasses because I was sure that I was in range of a normal eyed person's peripheral vision. Finally I said "Hello, I'm an architect and I'm in a hurry but I think I need some reading glasses". He slammed closed the book and said "great, I was just looking for an architect in the yellow pages, come inside". He needed some partition relocations, a rest room and a consultation room for his new practice. I designed his new office, got new reading glasses and even learned how to shape my new lenses in his grinding machine. A good start for both our practices.

4. PLACE MAT DESIGN:

Having a small office and a part-time secretary made it impossible to have time enough for business strategy sessions. In order to prolong her day and have the time to talk about the business we would occasionally have luncheon meetings when her meter wasn't running and we could be relatively undisturbed.

At one such luncheon a local contractor, who knew me, was in the restaurant talking to the Owner. He came over and introduced me to the Owner and asked if I could help. The Owner wanted a new canopy over his restaurant's entrance and the contractor was frustrated because he had been told that, even though the canopy was not an enclosed building, he would need drawings by an Architect, signed and sealed.

We discussed the canopy and I made Sketches on the back of an unused paper place setting from the next table. I drew very carefully and had the Owner looking over my shoulder to approve each stroke of my pencil. "That's perfect" he said, "can you sign and seal it"?

"Yes I can" I said, but you need three drawings for filing. Lunch was free that day and I went back to the office, printed three copies of the place mat, signed them, sealed them, and returned to a very grateful Owner. It was built just as I had drawn it.

Word got out to my fellow practitioners and I took a lot of ribbing for a few months, but I satisfied my client and had a good lunch too.

5. Variance After The Fact:

Projects do not always run easily. In fact, most have problems which have to be solved at sometime during the procedure.

I had been commissioned to do a small medical building in a downtown area and all was going well as the building was erected. About two weeks before final construction the neighbor in the building next to the construction notified the Local Building Inspector that the building was over the setback line and the construction should be stopped and partially torn down to eliminate the violation.

The Client, Contractor and I were all shocked with the news as we had taken steps at the beginning of the project to ensure that the work conformed to the Zoning Ordinance. It turns out that the complaining neighbor was a Land Surveyor who wanted the surveying job but was turned down by my client before the project even started.

The Surveyor who was used by my client used a point of two hundred feet away to establish the location of the property line. The neighbor was familiar with the City from his long time experience there and knew there was a discrepancy in the location of property lines. The City Engineer agreed with the neighbor and ruled that we were indeed two and a half feet in front of the setback line. Fortunately, we were not over the property line. The neighbor knew of the violation before the ground breaking but waited to get his revenge for not being hired until it was too late to correct the problem easily.

With a little diplomacy my Client and I convinced the City Fathers that we did not do this intentionally, could have corrected it if we were informed early enough and that the violation would not be detrimental to the Zoning Ordinance or Master Plan.

We applied for and received a Variance at a Public Meeting with only one objector. He left the meeting in a hurry not wanting to sustain any "bodily harm". His haste was not necessary as my client was a devout pacifist.

6. NOT ALL ARE PACIFISTS:

I was commissioned to do a Clothing Warehouse at the edge of town. When the drawings were completed I arranged to have local contractors provide sealed bids for the Construction Contract.

When the bids were open "Ahab", the contractor, was the low bidder and consequently selected to perform the work. The Building Permits were obtained and the work started.

As the Architect, I would visit the Construction Site once or twice a week. One morning I arrived and found the Contractor tired and out of sorts. I inquired about his condition and he related the following story:

The day before he had arrived at the site and all the concrete forms had been disrupted and the reinforcing bars were strewn all over the site. He was not a union contractor and had been warned that if he did not hire union workers he would be sorry. The disruption of the site was his penalty for not conforming. Not giving in to the demands, he instructed the crew to clean up the site, rearrange the forms and prepare for concrete delivery the next day.

He came to the site about 10:00 PM and waited in the dark with a loaded twelve gauge shotgun. At about two in the morning he saw headlights approaching the site. It stopped near the excavation and he saw the shadow of two men getting out. Fortunately, they were on the opposite side of the excavation because as they approached the excavation he fired both barrels in their direction. At that range the shots were too dispersed to do much damage. He saw them run to the vehicle and drive away. "I've been up all night", he said, "but they won't be back". I told him that "he was crazy to try such a stunt and that he could have hurt or killed someone". I can only wonder what he would have done to the Surveyor in the previous chapter.

7. GUNS AND BUILDINGS:

Although not seeming related, guns have played a part in my building recollections. I had one client who bought a building to house a truck maintenance operation. I was to design the interior space with offices, toilets and work bays for the trucks.

Before we could start on the project, the client came to me with a problem: While the building was in good shape structurally (I had given it my blessing before he purchased it), he had a new problem. The building had been unoccupied for a year or so before he purchased it. Through an inoperable exhaust fan, pigeons had found their way into the building and were nesting on and around the steel bar joist structural system.

For some very unwise reason he decided to shoot the pigeons with a 22 rifle. Unfortunately, he was a bad shot and gave up trying after several rounds had been fired. The first stage of construction was to fix the roof where the bullets had penetrated allowing the rain to come in.

Another gun related project was that I was commissioned to design a police and private pistol range in a rural area of a nearby town. The police and consequently the city fathers were in favor of this project because the police could train indoors where it would be safe for the surrounding community since their present range facility was outdoors.

The highlight of this project for me was a visit to the Port Authority Police Pistol Range which was located three stories below grade at the now destroyed World Trade Center Building. It was a very impressive visit and I learned a lot about combat police tactics and gun smoke ventilation.

8. STAFF:

Every successful Architect must have a supporting staff, which diligently and competently carry out the daily tasks of the profession. For the most part I have been fortunate with my personnel over the years. There have been some incidents which were memorable and I wish to relate them here.

9. ANTON:

One of my most productive draftsman was born and studied Architecture in a European country. He started working for me about five years after he left his original homeland.

Of course we had a language problem but his understanding of construction details and his European work ethic made him a valuable asset to my firm.

His weakness was the spelling and the grammar of the English language. As I was always responsible for the technical accuracy of the drawings produced in my office, I had to take extra precautions as I checked Anton's drawings. Such words, such as "cockcrete slab", "walking" closet" and "fritch plate" are some memorable examples. A "long span trust" is a great name for a bank but not applicable to Architectural engineering. Other substitutes were "fence drain" for "French drain" and "chain link French" for "chain link fence". I never recovered from "gotto way" for "cat walk".

10. GIUSEPPE:

Another staff member needed two weeks to recover from his circumcision. I don't know why he waited so long to have this done and I was shocked when he showed me his before and after photographs.

11. Schultz:

One memorable incident occurred when one of the draftsmen had an "all nighter" the night before. During our lunch break he decided to take a nap under his drafting table without telling anyone of his intention.

Upon returning to her drafting table after the lunch period, the gal at the next drafting table, saw the guy on the floor next to her position. He was fast asleep and she thought he was dead. Her screams could be heard throughout the office and we all ran to see what the commotion was about. He awoke at the same time the rest of the office converged at the scene. He was just as surprised as we all were and promised not to do it again. A few weeks later we found him sleeping on the front lawn.

12. LOUIE:

One of my management techniques is and always has been to maintain an "esprit de corps" with my staff. We always had "wine downs" on Friday afternoons to welcome in the weekends and planned office outings three or four times a year just to have fun and relax. I always closed the office during the State's Architects Convention and rented hotel rooms for the staff members who attended the convention and attended the educational meetings.

One of my favorite staff relaxing activities was to charter a bus and take them all to a professional baseball game. I would have the gals make lunch baskets for everyone and off we would go for our picnic and ball game. I would also bring my accordion along so we could have a "sing-along" during the before and after bus trips.

On one such outing all went well until we were loading the bus to return home. After we got on the bus and took attendance we noticed that "Louie" did not respond to our roll call. Several of the men went looking for him in the large parking lot which adjoined the ball park stadium. As time went by the lot emptied but no Louie turned up.

The bus driver, who was very cooperative, offered to drive around the lot to pick up the searchers and see if we could make our presence known to Louie. We drove all around the parking area but no Louie appeared. I was perplexed about what decision I should make as to whether we should leave without Louie. Did he have enough money to get transportation back? Was he in trouble with other spectators? Should I contact the police? Will the rest of the staff find fault with my decision, whatever it is?

As I was pondering the decision one draftsman hollered out "here's Louis". He was curled up in a bus seat sound asleep. What a relief. I was mad and glad at the same time. I went to awaken him and smelled the beer on his breath. He had obviously had too much to drink and no one knew that he slipped onto the bus and passed out.

Cheers went up and we started home without incident. There was no accordion music the way back as I and all my staff was exhausted from the hunting experience. We all remember that day and we refer to the trip as the "Looking for Louie Party".

13. Sady:

All offices need administrative support. Bookkeeping, filing, billing, typing, receptionists and personnel record keeping are all necessary support positions.

As the practice grew, so did the need for administrative support. At one point we needed a secretary-typist to assist in the chores. Calls were made and personnel were tested. One young lady was selected to become part of the staff and she was to report the following day.

She arrived on time but didn't seem to be "in the mood" for work. My administrative leader gave her a handwritten document to type with the instructions regarding headings, margins, spacing, indentations and the like. I might add that at the time the "computer" was not the main office machine that it is today.

The result of her first typing chore was a disaster. None of the above mentioned settings were correct. She was ordered to type it over and make the corrections. The second try was not much better than the first and she was ordered to do it again. The third try, while still not perfect, was accepted reluctantly. The new typist complained and stated "I hope you don't expect me to type this way every day". She never returned after lunch and would not have been remembered except that a week later she applied for unemployment benefits from my office. We won that case.

14. MUSIC IN ARCHITECTURE:

To my knowledge, not too much has been written about Architects who were musicians. The famous Frank Lloyd Wright may have been musically inclined but none of the Architects I know are musicians.

I play several instruments and use playing music to relax after a day's work. Even though I do not consider myself a professional musician I have used my skills to help my clients in their building projects.

I designed a restaurant and on opening day I attended with my accordion and helped make the opening a success. I was told that the returning customers asked "where's the accordionist"? Needless to say I enjoyed hearing about the inquiry.

15. Salvation:

My most memorial recollection regarding my music and my architecture occurred during a Christmas Season when I offered to play in an upscale shopping center for a Kettle Tender from The Salvation Army. I was designing a new Citadel for them and they always set-up Kettle Collections during the holidays.

I set up at the intersection of two main corridors with the Kettle nearby. In one hour we collected $375.00 which, I was told, was some sort of record.

The most memorable part of the event was that one of my previous clients saw me and came up to me to talk. I was dressed in my normal dress, a sweater and slacks, but it did not register to him hat I was only doing this as a favor to my present clients.

He said, "Jim, I'm sad to see that you've come on hard times". "Merry Christmas" I said to him as he put a twenty dollar bill in the Kettle. I'll never forget his generosity and the incident that day.

16. Dangerous and Unusual Clients:

As all Architects we deal with clients who find us in various ways. Some from other satisfied client's recommendations, some from the phone book, some from just walking in from the street.

I'll let you, the reader, judge who were dangerous or unusual. (Please remember that of the 3,000 clients mentioned above only a small percentage fill this category).

17. International:

A small man with a heavy Italian accent walked in the office. He had no appointment. "Senor Gaspari", he said, pronouncing my name the way it should be pronounced, are you an Architect"? Being aware of his obvious birthplace I said "Si".

"Good", he said, I want you to design a church for my "milk brother". "When I was a baby and my mother was breast feeding me, she was also nursing a baby boy whose mother could not nurse him. That's how he became my milk brother". He continued, "now he is a priest in Sicily and wants to build a new church. I've been a successful businessman in America and want to help him build his church". "Can you do this for me"? I nodded affirmatively and he smiled. "It has to be in Italian and under the metric system. Can you do it"? "Yes" I said knowing that I had two people on staff of Italian decent.

We agreed on a price and he gave me a deposit and left a happy man. My staff, who heard the initial comments, came to me laughing. "How can we do this, we don't know how to speak Italian"? "But your parents do", I said, "they can help". No they can't, they can't write in Italian, they had no schooling in Italy before they came here". What a dilemma. A local contractor came to the rescue and I did the metric conversion.

The client would come in every week to see the progress of the drawings bringing with him dates, olives and grapes for the staff. We all benefited from this client.

18. Crash Time:

Having designed a legal office for a downtown area building, I was on an inspection visit close to the time when the construction would complete. Everything seemed okay until I heard some banging and metal to metal contact from one of the Central Consultation Offices. I entered the room and found the client's wife swinging an automobile snow tire chain against an expensive walnut finished wall. "What are you doing"?, I inquired. "I'm distressing the wood paneling. I told my husband that I wanted distressed walnut finish in his office". "He never mentioned it to me", I said. "I could have specified distressed walnut to be installed". "He never listens to me" she said, "but now he will".

I left in a hurry but heard the banging all the way into the parking lot. My client never mentioned his new paneling to me so I guess he learned to live with it. My fee was paid in full.

19. Stage Fright:

One client whom I'll never forget called up and inquired if I would design a house addition. After telling her that I would, she asked me if I would visit her at 7:00 a.m.. "Why so early" I asked, and her answer was reasonable. "I understand that Frank Lloyd Wright would live with his clients for a while before he would design something for them so he could get the full measure of how they lived". Having been "challenged" to do a "F.L.W. thing" I couldn't say "no".

We arranged a date and I arrived at 6:55 a.m.. (I'm always early for my appointments). Her husband let me in and directed me to the kitchen table where there were five places set. Two children came down from upstairs and sat down. I questioned where the lady of the house is and was told she will be soon.

From the stairway came the ringing of a servant's dinner bell and she appeared wearing a tutu and a blinking flashlight. She said "Do you know who I am"? I was speechless. "Can't you tell I'm Tinkerbell"?, she advised. I was still speechless. She continued "one day each week I dress up for breakfast and ask the kids to guess my identity". "Last week I was Peter Pan and before that I was Little Miss Muffet and before that I was Alice in Wonderland". "I don't want my children to take me for granted so I dress up to be something special so they will remember me". "How unusual I thought".

She continued, "So I want the addition to my house to have an elevated runway so I can do my act and be seen". I think this was the first time that the husband heard about the runway and not surprisingly, after that initial encounter, the project never went ahead. It was one of the most unusual meetings I ever had.

20. Slipping In:

The second most unusual meeting occurred a few years later when I was invited to a Doctor's home for an interior renovation. Because my wife was an Interior Decorator, I invited her to come with me as I felt her services might be needed as well. When we arrived I was greeted at the door by a beautiful woman who I estimated was in her mid twenties. She was wearing nothing but a tight fitting tee shirt which revealed a well developed upper body leaving nothing to the imagination. I didn't have the nerve to inspect what she wore on the bottom.

"Are you Mrs. Smith"? I asked. "No" she replied "I am the governess". "Wow" I thought. "Mrs. Smith and Doctor Smith are inside waiting to meet you".

Mrs. Smith was a very attractive woman, too. After exchanging greetings Dr. Smith explained their needs. "We want our children to play inside our house when the weather is inclement". "We want you to design a slide in our living room which will go to the basement so they can play".

It didn't take me long to reply that, while this is possible, the construction would tend to deflate the value of their house if it ever went for resale. "I'm not thinking of resale at this time, but

I do have three conditions to the construction that you must address". "Of course Doctor, please tell me" I answered. He continued "the basement has a hard concrete floor and I want you to make sure that the kids will have a soft landing".

My wife, having been listening to the conversations, chimed in "we can install a couch that folds into a flat mattress, when opened, that would fit well under the slide but which could be set up as a couch when the slide wasn't being used". They both responded well to her suggestion.

"The second condition", he added, "is that the slide has to be enclosed so that the kids can't fall off on the way down and hurt themselves on the hard concrete floor". "No problem", I answered as I envisioned bent steel rod and canvas covering to enclose the slide.

"What is the third condition"?, I asked. The answer was a shocker. "It has to be large enough for adults", he said. My wife and I were so shocked at the last condition that we don't remember how we ended our meeting and left the house. I suppose I told them that I would send him a Proposal for my services to confirm our agreement. I never sent him a Proposal because shortly after our visit I read in the local newspaper that he had committed suicide.

21. X Rated:

Another encounter that is memorable occurred in a small neighboring town where I was commissioned to design and supervise the construction of an addition to a living room and dining room in a rather small house.

Everything went well and as I made my final visit to sign-off on the addition, the housewife asked since she was happy with the addition, could I help her in the bedroom. "Sure", I said, "let me see the problem". She ushered me into her bedroom, which was brightly lit by the spring time sunlight. The windows were open and they had by-parting draperies which matched the bed spread. I could see no problem with the room. "What's wrong"? I asked. She answered it's not conducive, my husband and I don't make love any more". "You should see a therapist" was my immediate response. "No" she said, "I thought you could help me". At that I was beginning to get the gist of her wishes. I could feel the perspiration dripping from my arm pits as I was sure of her intentions. "I'm sorry, I can't help you" I said, and left hastily. I deposited the final payment she had just given me before she might change her mind since I was uncooperative in the end and returned to the office and sat alone in silence.

Two weeks later she called and complained about a roof leak and would like me to come and look at it. I said that I would call the contractor and have him make the repair since he had a year's guarantee on his work as per the Construction Contract I had written for her. I called the contractor and he promised to fix the leak.

Two weeks later she called again and complained about her leaky roof. "Didn't the contractor come to fix the leak" I asked. "Yes, but it still leaks", she said. I told her I would call him again. I called and told his answering machine that "the roof still leaked".

Two weeks went by and she called again with the same complaint. "Did the contractor come again" I asked. "Yes, but it still leaks" she said. I was angered by the unsuccessful repair of such a nice and well received project and I feared that the client might find fault with my design. This time I called and the contractor answered. "What's the matter with you"? I demanded, "can't you fix this lady's roof"? He replied "What roof, she's fantastic". It all came together to me at his answer as I remembered by last meeting with her. "For God's sake man, give her your phone number so I don't have to be the "middle man" any more. He laughed, agreed, and hung up. I never heard from either of them since.

22. Catherine and the Boy Scout:

I was called to design an addition to a religious building. Upon arriving at the first Building Committee meeting I met Catherine, the Committee Chairwoman. She seemed overly happy to meet me and she smiled at me constantly.

The project went along smoothly and all the Staff and Committee seemed well pleased with my design and the job went into construction without much problem. There were many night time Committee Meetings and Catherine was always friendly and supportive of my Design.

We went out for Construction Bids and the "Boy Scout" and his construction company was the low bidder and selected to do the work. Catherine seemed happy with the selection of the contractor and gave a warm welcome to the "Boy Scout". The project went smoothly as we all got along well. The addition was a two story structure of classrooms and offices and a renovation of the Nave. There were also barrier free toilets for the Staff and Congregation and an elevator connecting the two floors. When the project was completed, the Clergyman established a dedication for the new construction with all the Staff, Congregations, Contractor and Architect.

Naturally I attended and asked my wife to join me in what I thought would be a pleasant affair and one that she would enjoy. She had become friendly with Catherine during the construction as they had some interfacing with the decorating of the new building. All three of us sat together in the front row and listened to the dedication proceedings. Much to our surprise the preaching centered on infidelity and misconduct. What was more surprising was that the Clergyman kept looking at me and Catherine as he continued.

I turned to my wife and said that this was a strange topic to pick at a dedication and we continued to pay attention to the sermon from the pulpit. After the ceremony, we had a brief time at a small buffet and I explained my surprise to my wife and Catherine at the topic of the dedication sermon. Catherine smiled and said "that's him and don't worry about it".

Several weeks later I was told by the contractor that Catherine and the Boy Scout had run away together and that his father threatened to disown him if he didn't return home to his wife and family.

The Boy Scout returned home and at our next encounter he explained what happened. As the construction neared completion Catherine wanted to walk the project with the Boy Scout. As they toured the building she wanted to try the elevator. Once inside the elevator with the door closed she hit the red switch and stopped the elevator between floors. And, in his words, "she jumped me".

He then admitted that he was very amused at the dedication because he surmised that the clergyman must have heard about the elevator incident and assumed that it was the Architect in the elevator instead of him. It all made sense to me and I was freed from my guilt for an incident I didn't commit. We still talk about the elevator incident but I haven't been back in the building since the dedication.

23. Chinese Party:

It has become quite common to have women running for local political office. While there is no problem with their ability to preside over the affairs of their office, their gender has raised some embarrassing moments for their staffs. The following was told to me by the "Hero".

In one town, which had a female Mayor, the men on her staff unwittingly created such a moment. The Township had evening monthly meetings for their Planning Board and Zoning Board. This is as most towns do as it's difficult to get full public attendance during normal working hours.

What was different in this Town, however, was that the male staff who had to attend these meetings, decided at some point in time, to stay overnight in a local hotel to avoid driving home in the wee hours of the morning the next day, only to rise again too soon and commute back to their jobs at the Town Hall.

While they had a good excuse not to return to their homes when they were needed at the Town Hall, their excuse degenerated to "a great night" with the boys. One of the men suggested and arranged for some women from a local escort service to meet the guys at the hotel after the meeting. Naturally this was a clandestine operation and secrecy was of paramount importance.

During the afternoon preceding the monthly night meeting, the instigator of this illicit operation called his fellow staff members to determine just how many participants would be interested in an escort for the after meeting meeting. The code word was "Chinese". "Do you want any Chinese tonight"? When the tally was known, the hero would make the arrangements with the time, place and number information for the escort service. This seemed to work efficiently for a while. No one ever expected that the Mayor would call for a meeting after working hours requiring the staff to stay late to listen to some administration changes that she was contemplating. She felt it was good leadership to express her thoughts to her Staff and get their reactions to her changes before she implemented them.

Realizing that she would be detaining her Staff on a day when there wasn't any night time meetings, knowing that they would miss dinner, as the meeting started she decided to arrange for some food to be brought in. She asked with all good intention "Do you want any Chinese tonight? She was overwhelmed the laughter and smiles she received from her thoughtful and innocent question. "What's so funny", she asked. Our "hero", realizing that this was a very serious moment answered with "oh, it's just an inside joke" followed by "thank you for thinking about us: Chinese will be fine". This close call was too much for the participants and the hero told me that their secret practice died on the meeting/dinner table that evening.

I don't know whether the Mayor ever found out about the real meaning of "Chinese" but this story lives on in my memory as well as in the memory of those participants who needed a "night out with the boys".

24. VODKA WATER:

The sexual side of Architecture recurs again. While designing a building for a nationally known company, which had only female real estate and construction executors at the New Jersey site, I was ordered to visit its national headquarters in a southern state. Both Sam the Contractor and I were invited.

The arrangements were made and we flew down in the morning and returned that same day. When we arrived we were met by one of the executive officers. She was a young woman, neatly tailored, and very attractive. When we arrived at headquarters we were surprised by all the young and attractive women who made up the majority of the staff. The office boys were really boys, but the CEO of the company was male. On the return trip, Sam and I discussed the staffing situation and at the very next meeting, at the job site, I asked the female real estate executive, if she could explain the predominance of attractive female executives in the corporate offices as well as the female managers on the construction site. The answer was astonishing but logical. Because of the nature of the business, telephone operators made up the majority of the personnel. As the business grew, the CEO wanted to repay and acknowledge all the efforts of all the dedicated phone operators which made his business a huge success.

Since the company was growing at a fast rate, he decided to elevate his trusted phone operators to executive positions. Being Southern Belles they maintained their attractive looks. As the job progressed there were a number of complaints from various workmen on the site that the women supervisors were the most difficult they had ever encountered. At one meeting on the site, that the women were not in attendance, one workman took me aside to cite his frustration. He stated that in all his experience as a construction worker he had never been scolded or threatened in the manner in which this woman supervisor had spoken. She said that "if I didn't correct the installation of the wiring she would cut my balls off. No other construction supervisor had ever threatened me like that".

I calmed him down and met with Sam to discuss the matter. Sam knew of other such incidents and we decided to bring it to the main woman on the project. She assured us that this was a result of the rapid development of phone operators being quickly advancing to executive managerial positions. "They are acting as they perceive their male counterparts acted in similar situations". She agreed to speak to her subordinates to try and tone down the language to something more in keeping with the tradition of construction management used by male supervisors.

My observations made me realize that she, as well as the other women on this project, were acting as they felt their male counterparts acted. One incident that proved my observations to be correct happened at the Christmas Party.

All the women and the subcontractor supervisors were invited to attend a Christmas party to be given by the client at a local restaurant. Sam and I were also invited. There were about twenty-five people in total. During the afternoon of the party day, I spoke to Sam to make sure he knew about the party and would attend. I did not want to be alone with the head woman as she had requested that I accompany her at the head table. He assured me that he was going to attend.

I met the "Boss' lady at the appropriate time and she ushered me to a seat next to her. She asked me what I wanted to drink and I answered "Vodka". "Get yourself vodka and get me a scotch and soda" she requested. I did as she requested and took my assigned seat next to her.

In what seemed like only a few minutes she asked me again for another scotch and soda. I got her another drink and returned to my seat. Dinner was served. "Is Sam coming tonight" she asked. "I spoke to him this afternoon and he said he was", I answered.

By this time I had finished my vodka and she ordered another scotch. I was watching the door looking for Sam to enter. Then she said to me, "If Sam doesn't show up I'm taking you home with me tonight". I wasn't shocked but disturbed that my fears, although unfounded, were coming true. I needed to think fast.

I took her glass and mine and went to the bar. I ordered a scotch and soda for her and went to the men's room to fill my glass with water. I returned to my seat and handed her her third scotch.

It wasn't long before she requested a fourth scotch. I had observed her drinking intervals and took a sip of water from my glass at the same time she took her sips. Both glasses got emptied at the same time and I had guessed she wanted another. "These women are crazy if they think men drink so much" I thought to myself and said "I wonder what happened to Sam". It doesn't matter she said, you are here".

I came back to my seat with her fourth drink and my glass of water. At an appropriate time I braced my body with both hands on the table and said "I think I'm going to throw-up. I have to leave, I don't feel well". She was stunned by my apparent inability to hold my liquor and got up and turned her attention elsewhere. I left immediately without saying good-by.

The next day I called Sam and told him what had happened and asked where he had been. Without seeing his expression, I knew he was smiling and said "I had something else to do". I was happy that it only cost me four scotches and two vodkas to keep me out of trouble. She never talked about the incident again and the job finished smoothly.

25. ALCOHOL CONTRACT:

It was at the beginning of construction on a large warehouse in my local area. The General Contractor had received his building permit and the excavation subcontractor was scheduled to start. A.B.C. Excavating Company had been hired by the General Contractor who had used this company on a prior job for the same Owner. I was satisfied with A.B.C.'s work in the past and, as a courtesy to the excavator and a responsibility to my client, I made my usual "first day" visit to the site.

When I arrived at 7:00 a.m., I saw bull dozers, back hoes and dump trucks parked on the site ready for action. I was happy to see all the equipment until I noticed that the name painted on the door of the dump trucks was "Joe's Excavating". Joe's Excavating Company was also local and had been used on some of my projects so my first thought was that A.B.C. had asked Joe's to help him do the project.

What seems now to be a stupid question I went up to the driver of the lead dump truck and asked "Are you working for A.B.C."? I received a curt and surprising answer, "Can't you see the name on my truck? I work for Joe's Excavating". "How could this be", I thought, "The General Contractor had told me he hired A.B.C.".

There wasn't a phone, as yet, on the site and this was before cell phones became a tool of necessity. I jumped into my car and rode to the nearest pay phone. I called the General Contractor and inquired about his subcontractor. He was as surprised as I, and reaffirmed that his contractor was A.B.C.. I suspected that my client had something to do with this. I got back in my car and drove to my client's office. I stormed into the office and demanded to see the Boss. In a few moments his second in command entered the Reception Room wearing a "smile of sympathy". He put his arm around me and said "I think I know why you're here. You've been to the site, haven't you"? I nodded yes and he said "Have a seat". He continued "Last night the Boss and I were having dinner at our favorite "watering hole" and Joe from Joe's Excavating came in and sat at the next table. Joe bought the Boss a few drinks and they talked over old times as they had been friends as young men".

I knew what was coming, but I kept quiet and listened. He continued "Joe said he had come upon hard times and that work was slow and he needed a job very soon to keep him in business. By the end of the meal they were both under the influence and shock hands and the Boss told him that he should start tomorrow on my project. All this happened without notice to me or the General Contractor and as far as my client was concerned, he wanted Joe to do the excavating and since he was the Boss, he could do what he wanted without any interference from me or the General Contractor.

I calmed down a little and quietly said that the Boss had violated his contract with the General Contractor and that I would see if there was a solution to the problem.

I met with the General Contractor and the Owner of A.B.C. Excavating the following day. A.B.C. wanted $5,000.00 to release his subcontract with the General Contractor. I called the second in command and he agreed to the settlement.

My Owner learned a lesson and accepted the fact that his wonderful dinner with his "old friend" cost $5,000.00 more than the meal and the tip.

26. COSTLY MISCONCEPTIONS:

Designing and constructing a religious building is always filled with personal and emotional problems. While one might think that custom home projects head the list of projects with these problems, my experience has proven otherwise. In a private house project, the Owners, husbands and wives, are usually on the "same page" in the play book with only minor disagreements on color or décor. In Religious Architecture the views of the congregants are known only to themselves without the knowledge of how the other congregant thinks about their religion or what different views of what and how should be done to enhance the religious experience. To work in this void the administration of a construction project requires extensive experience and knowledge. The Architect must take on the role of artist, teacher and therapist to accomplish a successful project. A project which pushed me to the task of this triad was an addition to a Religious Building not very far from my office.

A congregant, who was a former client of mine, was a plumbing contractor. I had designed his new office building and storage building a few years before. He recommended me to the Building Committee and after an interview I was awarded the Contract to Design and Administer the Construction.

I knew that Hank, the plumber, was interested in doing the plumbing on the project, but I let it be known that the project would be competitively bid by general contractors who would select their subcontractors before they handed in their bids. They usually select the lowest bidders, if their prices aren't unreasonably low due to some miscalculation on their part in the bidding process.

Hank asked me who the general contractors were bidding the project. I gave this information out to any subcontractor who is looking for work and inquires about the bidders. This is an effort to get the best price possible for my clients.

During the bidding time there are many rumors flying around as to who is bidding what job and who needs work badly. It was no secret that Hank was a member of the congregation and was going to bid. At the same time the Building Committee Chairman asked another plumber he met at a social function if he knew about the project and if he was bidding it. The Chairman also knew the importance of having multiple bidders in the same trade to achieve the lowest price. The answer he received was "that's Hank's job, I'd be wasting my time bidding".

The Chairman misconstrued the reply to mean that Hank had told all his fellow plumbers that he was going to get the job regardless of what their bids were. I did not hear of this conversation until the day of the bidding but the Chairman decided that Hank was fixing the bids in his favor.

The bids were received on the appropriate day and time and were opened by the Building Committee in private. The low bidder was interviewed and was asked who the low plumber bidder was. His answer was "Hank, but he was the only bidder". The Chairman was furious. He told the contractor that if he wanted the job he had to get a different plumber.

I objected to the stipulation because I understood that it would be difficult to get new plumbing bids in time for our proposed ground breaking date and I didn't think that Hank had personally talked to all the plumbers and asked them not to bid. I thought that at the very worst, Hank would try to find out what the lowest plumbing price was and try to match or beat it in negotiations with the winning contractor. I believe to this day that he didn't know he was the only plumbing bidder. The contractor asked "how can I get another bidder. They all know that Hank will be standing in the wings waiting to match their price". I spoke to the Chairman regarding my objection to this procedure and told him he would have to guarantee that the new plumber would get the job if he took the time and energy to give a responsible bid. He agreed with hesitation and he informed the contractor.

We missed the ground breaking day but had the ceremony on time. A week and a half later the general contractor arrived in my office with a new plumbing bid. It was close to Hanks bid although a little bit higher. I told the contractor to sign him up and start work with a slightly higher price. I had no choice as I had given a guarantee.

When Hank found out that he had been replaced, he was furious with me. I told him to meet with me and I would explain how this happened and how I gave my "word" to the general contractor. He refused to meet with me but requested a meeting with the Board of Trustees. They agreed to meet with him without my attendance.

The Chairman came to me the day after the meeting and told me about the meeting. Hank was literally in tears and claimed that after all the work that he had done in the past for no compensation he was saddened that his fellow congregants would betray him when he tried to do the best for them.

The Chairman told me that the Board had agreed with Hank and that I should tell the contractor to void his contract with the other plumber and make him give the contract to Hank. I refused at first for obvious reasons but thought I might have a solution. I contacted the general contractor and told him to find a manner of compensation to the second plumber for not taking the project even though he had my guarantee and had expended time to bid the project plumbing. I knew that he had done work on the bidding because his price was very close to the bid that Hank had provided.

The answer came back the next day. The second plumber wanted $10,000.00 not to sign the contract. I presented this to the Chairman. He went back to the Board for their vote. They decided it wasn't worth $10,000.00 to give Hank the job.

The project went ahead without Hank. Hank resigned from the congregation and never spoke to me again or bid any of my projects. The lesson is that emotions run high on religious projects, perhaps more than we think. The whole incident would have passed had not the Chairman misunderstood the gossip that occurred during the bidding.

27. TENNIS ANYONE:

Alcohol and Architecture do not mix well but occasionally it makes for an interesting story. I had designed a house for another client who also used the evening dinner hour for his contract negotiations.

In this episode my client advised me in advance that he wanted his friend Bob, the Heating Contractor, to be the one selected for the Heating and Air Conditioning Contract. I had Designed a Two Zone Gas Fired Forced Air Heating and Cooling System. Bob, being an old friend of the client, wanted to improve on my Design by using two different systems, hot water for heating and forced air for cooling. I admitted that the suggested change was a better system but more expensive and that it was the client's decision if he didn't mind the extra cost.

A few drinks and the two of them came to an equitable additional cost and all was well, almost. When we got up from the dinner table I noticed that both of them started to stagger.

I was not so stable myself, but I recovered quickly as I helped my client to negotiate around the other tables in the dining room. I had had only two drinks but they had consumed four or five each. Sensing that they should not drive I ordered them into my car so that I could drive them home.

I didn't know where Bob lived, but I knew where my client lived, and he knew where Bob lived. "You can pick up your cars tomorrow", I said, as I gently pushed and pulled my two companions into my car. I owned a 1957 Volkswagen Bug at the time and the scene reminded me of a circus act in reverse. They got in and since they were both about 6 feet tall they spread out and filled the inside completely

The trip was much more than I anticipated because they could not remember the direction to John's house. They directed me to one area and I pulled into what they said was his driveway. I opened Bob's door and he leaned his head out and looked around. "This ain't my house" he said and slumped back in the back seat.

Finally after a few more incorrect turns we arrived at Bob's house. His wife met us with hands on her hips as if she knew what happened. My guess was that this was not the first time he had been driven home. She thanked me and escorted him into their house. I easily found my way to my client's house and then to my home.

My feeling of satisfaction with the incident vanished quickly as I was greeted by my wife as I entered my house. "Where have you been"? she asked, "you stink". "Don't you know you are playing tennis tonight with the guys"? "I'm o.k." I said, and explained that I was the only sober guy in the crowed. "You can't drive to the courts tonight, whose in your group? I will call for one of them to pick you up". She had made her decision and picked up the phone.

They picked me up as she had arranged and told them of my condition. I didn't have any trouble changing into my tennis clothes and wondered why she reacted so strongly upon my condition.

We talked about unrelated subjects during the 15 minute drive to the tennis courts and I didn't feel any sense of the effects of the two drinks that I had. We warmed up at our assigned court at the assigned time and chose which partners would be which for our doubles match. We changed partners each week and it didn't matter to me with whom I would be playing.

We started playing and I always let my partner serve first when it was our service. I took my place at the net. The first return of service came right at me and I smashed a winner. I did the same on the next three services. Without thinking or straining, I dominated the whole match, running wildly, hitting winners from all parts of the court. Smashing backhands and forehands, which not only surprised my fellow players but also myself. In retrospect I had never played so well before this match and I never played so well since. When they returned me home they asked my wife, "what did you give him for dinner"? She smiled and said "ask his client".

I haven't had a drink before any tennis game since that night, but I think I should have.

28. $20,000 KISS:

It's not only the Architects who have problems with amorous inclinations of their clients. One incident which will not escape my memory occurred at the end of a million dollar addition project in New Jersey.

It was several days before Christmas and the Contractor and I were meeting with Thelma, the Building Committee Chairwoman, to discuss the approval of the final twenty thousand dollar balance owed to the Contractor as the final payment.

The meeting was very cordial and both she and I were pleased with the final result of the addition. He was all smiles as I told him that I was approving the work and he should get his final payment before the end of the year. I excused myself and left the building.

The next day I got a call from the Contractor. "I just left the police station and I must talk to you", he said. I replied with "What happened"? "When you left yesterday I wished Thelma a Merry Christmas and tried to kiss her on the cheek. She had turned suddenly and I ended up missing her cheek and landed my kiss behind her ear. She was startled but didn't say anything. She moved away from me and quickly left the room. I only wanted to show friendship but I left the room a few seconds later".

"This morning I was in my office when the police came and arrested me for sexually assaulting Thelma. Apparently she took offense at my misplaced kiss and filed a complaint at police headquarters. I told them it was an honest sign of thanks and friendly affection and nothing more". The police weren't interested in my comments. Can you help me"?

"What can I do"? I said, "I left before the incident and didn't witness anything, but I will talk to Thelma and see what I can do". I called Thelma and got her side of the story. She felt that he was waiting for me to leave so that he could attack her. She did not trust him and decided that he was after her. There was nothing I could do to quiet her nerves and an apology was not enough to quell her anguish about the incident. She would not drop the charges.

The rest of her Committee was notified of the incident and they were shocked as well. One member of the Committee was a lawyer who suggested a solution: If the Contractor would forget the final $20,000.00 she should drop the charges.

Reluctantly she agreed and the matter was solved. The Contractor didn't want any bad publicity or wasting time on a criminal trial whose outcome was not certain since it was a "he said, she said" situation, and there were no witnesses.

We are all working normally again, but whenever I see him, I remind him of his $20,000.00 kiss.

29. Doctor: I have a Lady in the Balcony:

An Architect must serve his clients to the best of his ability. Sometimes it's difficult to maintain a professional image when the client's wishes are close to being pornographic. My position was "As long as it's not illegal, I'll do my job as best I can, trying to design the space without getting emotionally involved".

This was the situation with Dr. Havelook. After a frightful separation and divorce with his first wife, the good doctor married his head nurse. I did not know nor did I ask if his second wife played any part of his divorce. I didn't need to know and I didn't want to know as I wanted to keep my concerns with the new project the Doctor had in mind and not form any negative opinions of either the Doctor or his wife as I tried to solve their design problem.

Our first meeting was an eye opener as the program developed as follows: "We want to build a new master bedroom suite on the Doctor's existing house". "There are special details that must be included". We want a heart shaped bath tub recessed in the floor of the new bedroom. The new master bathroom will have a shower enclosed in glass, a double sink set into a granite countertop, a noise free water closet and a bidet. The door to the master bath will be a tiled arch with a pre-cast stone key stone".

The ceiling shall be high enough for the placement of a balcony with a ships ladder access stair. On the balcony will be electrically controlled lounge chairs which can be set to a multiple set of desired positions. At one end of the room there will be a white wall with no imperfections so it can be used as a projection screen to receive the images from a VCR projector located on the opposite side of the balcony. There should be a brass railing at the balcony edge to prevent people from falling off the balcony but the top railing must terminate in a pole similar to the fireman's pole so that fast access to the heart shaped bed is accomplished before the passion of the moment is not diminished by a lengthy and/or cumbersome decent.

I know the reader is smiling at this "wish list" but I can tell you that I kept a straight face throughout the program's disclosure. After the wife left the room the doctor shared with me his library of triple "X" rated video tapes to make sure I knew what the intent of the program was. I think his revelation of the tapes was his way of being sure that I knew their wishes apparently because, with some effort, I had not showed any emotion when hearing the details of their program. I must admit however, that when I explained the program to my staff I was much less pan-faced.

30. Non-Compatibilities:

Through my experiences I have come to know how to handle the marital problems of my clients. At the very outset I advise a couple of the facts of matrimony and construction. If the intent of an addition is to bring a separated couple together, forget about it. Just as having a baby to save marital problems doesn't work, neither can an Architect, as clever as he may be, improve a relationship between a husband and wife. In fact, a happily married couple ends up having difficulty when they embark on a construction project which changes their life styles.

Our project which proves my case is the new home I designed for David and Sally, a seemingly happy couple. They had no children but each had a successful business.

They purchased a beautiful lot in an upper middleclass neighborhood and asked me to design their dream house.

The problem was that each had different dreams. When I asked my usual personal questions it was obvious that I would have a problem satisfying both of them. He wanted an atrium in the center of the house in which he would plant a full grown tree. Her best wish was that she should be able to bathe nude outside in the fresh air where no one could see her. It was obvious to me that these items should not be located in the same area. My final design consisted of a center atrium which all the rooms of the home surrounded, each having a view of the fully grown tree. The private bath area was located on the outside of the house perimeter enclosed in glass with a glass top roof and a 7' high solid fence located 5' from the glass exterior wall which encircled the tub area. The shower stall was not a part of the tub enclosure but inside her bedroom complex.

At the completion of the project, David came into my office to make his final fee payment. He told me that he didn't move into his new home but that Sally did. They had separated and he remained in his old house.

31. APART TOGETHER:

Mrs. Smith called me from her house in an up-scaled neighborhood where I had some previous home addition projects. She had been talking to some friends abut me and wanted me to meet with her and her husband to discuss an addition to their home.

The date was set on a weekday afternoon when Mr. Smith, who was a CEO of a successful company, could make time for a meeting.

I am usually punctual and when I arrived Mrs. Smith greeted me warmly but with a look of desperation. "My husband just called, he's on his way but will be a little late. It's just as well as I need to talk to you before he arrives". She ushered me into the kitchen and motioned me in a chair with my back to the window. She sat opposite me so that she could see the driveway, obviously to know when he arrives. I took notice of this because my experience has taught me that separate conversations with one of the couples on a building project means that the two are not in agreement on part or the whole program of the project.

"My husband and I are separated but he promises to move back in if we do an addition to our house which will allow him to have a separate bedroom". I thought this would be a change; usually couples separate after the house addition that they intended to save a marriage didn't achieve their purpose.

She continued, "Money is not a concern as my husband can afford it, but I want him back as soon as possible". Her eyes shifted to the driveway and she stood up to open the door.

Mr. Smith was a handsome man with a good physic and slightly grey sideburns. He strode in confidently and shook my hand with a good grip. This was a well-to-do successful business man. He sat down next to me and told me the program.

"I want you to design an addition to the house to include the following: A good sized bedroom with a fully equipped bathroom. The bathroom should be placed next to the existing master bathroom. There should be a doorway from the new bathroom to the master bath to give me access to her bedroom". I kept listening but contained my smile as I remembered my tour through Versailles many years earlier as the King had his special door to the Queen's room. He continued "The most important part of the design is that I must have a separate entrance to my new room. This is to allow me to come and go without disturbing my wife who likes to sleep late in the morning".

We settled on the fee quickly and I left telling him that I would mail my detailed contract the next day for signing. "I'll come to your office to pick it up", she said. "Call me when it's ready".

I would measure the existing conditions and develop Preliminary Drawings within the next week and receive approval of the design in the following week. The final drawings took another two weeks and the contractor's bidding was eliminated since Mrs. Smith knew which contractor she wanted for the project. They signed him up and construction started. She was obviously pleased with the speed of the project.

Since the bedrooms were situated on the second floor, the addition had to be two stories. The lower floor was an entrance vestibule with a coat closet and a stair to the second floor new bedroom. The foundations were poured quickly and the framing followed immediately. It was a record pace for this type of project and Mrs. Smith was pleased at the progress.

Since there was no need for an addition to the basement, the first floor was designed as a concrete slab on-grade with a ceramic tile floor finish. The slab was poured as soon as the two story framing was complete.

Before the gypsum board could be installed, the electric wiring and the heating and air conditioning ductwork had to be installed. Mrs. Smith called me in a panic. "The contractor had an accident", she said. "He was doing some work on the first floor ceiling and fell off the ladder. He hit his head on the concrete and became unconscious. Can you come quickly"? "I'll be right there", I said, and left my office. When I arrived about 20 minutes later she met me in the driveway crying. "They took him away in an ambulance and he never woke up".

That afternoon I received the notice that the contractor, a man in his mid fifties, has succumbed as a result of a skull fracture. Mrs. Smith was inconsolable. "We must get a new contractor right away to continue the job. I want my husband back".

I met with Johnny, the second in command of the project, and asked him if he could continue the work. He was willing but I wanted him to be licensed, and insured, and to sign a

Construction Contract for the balance of the work for a price that would consider the work already accomplished and paid for. This procedure took several weeks and Mrs. Smith called me every day. I even got a call from Mr. Smith who wanted to meet me at the site.

I met with Mr. Smith and of course Mrs. Smith came outside after she saw two cars in her driveway. Mr. Smith quieted her as he defended the time delay and said that I was doing the right thing for their protection. Unhappily she went back into her house and Mr. Smith escorted me to my car which was parked next to his. He looked into the kitchen window to see if his wife was looking at us. Apparently she wasn't as he put one arm around me and shook my hand. "good job", he said as I felt something being placed in my right hand. "Keep it slow", he said, and got into his car. I looked at my hand and saw a one hundred dollar bill. I was surprised but put the bill in my pocket. I could justify keeping the tip because I did spend a lot of time getting the new contractor to finish the work while protecting my clients, but I also knew the message that he was not in a hurry to have the job finished so that he had to move back into the house.

The job did get completed as designed with good workmanship and Mrs. Smith was very happy. I never saw Mr. Smith again so I cannot report that the project was successful. My guess is that they are still "apart together".

32. THE THREE CLOWNS:

I was commissioned to design and supervise a large private home located on a lot off of a rural street which backed onto a fresh water lake. The lot was about a half acre and the land sloped about 10' from the front to the lake. The lake was part of the local reservoir system, and restricted to only electrically powered motor boats or sail boats. It was a beautiful lot indeed.

The program required four bedrooms and three bathrooms with kitchen, dining room, a large living room with a wood burning fireplace and a full basement with access to grade at the rear.

The Owners were a married couple who had two young children and were successful in the family business. Having a pleasant life style was more important than the cost of the project. This turned out to be both good and bad. The good part was that I didn't have to worry about my design meeting a pre-established budget. The bad part was that my clients selected contractors to build the house without bidding the project or doing a serious review of past projects or performances. Two weeks after the drawings were completed they introduced me to the Circus Brothers, Meany, Minie and Moe.

They were pleasant fellows and were very attentive to my instructions regarding the details of construction that I wanted followed. I thought they were clearly indicated on the drawings but I considered them crucial for a custom house.

The first detail I wanted them to follow was the method of excavation. I wanted the excavation to be dug vertically at the foundation walls so that no backfill would be placed against the foundation that was excavated by a sloping of the outside grade. This is because the backfilling of such an excavation puts horizontal pressure on the new foundation which may put the foundation out of plumb.

Another reason is that the compaction of the backfill will result in compaction not equaling the natural compaction of undisturbed soil. The result is a saucer shaped excavation which captures the rainwater in the backfilled soil and, because the undisturbed soil is less porous than the backfill, the storm water seeps through the backfill and flows on the top of the undisturbed soil toward the foundation creating a horizontal hydrostatic pressure on the foundation. This is not good if one is looking forward to a dry basement.

The second detail I insisted on is a footing drain on the outside of the exterior footing which will catch any storm water which gets over the foundation wall. Because the lot backs up to the lake, I designed the footing drain to extend to the rear to have the rainwater and the rain leaders empty into the lake. The level of the lake surface water was at least three feet below the bottom of the footings.

Meany asked me if we should have a footing drain on the inside of the house to catch any water that infiltrated under the basement slab. An emphatic "no" was my answer. There should not be any water under the slab if the exterior footing drain was installed properly.

The Owner heard my conversation with the brothers and was content with the dialogue and the job proceeded. A few days later I visited the site to see how the excavation was going. The three brothers were standing on the edge of the excavation scratching their heads and looking down into the pit they had dug. I came up to them and immediately knew their problem. The excavation was dug exactly as I had demanded. The excavation was about 8' deep with the outer walls perfectly plumb as I had requested. The problem that perplexed the Clown Brothers was that the back-hoe, which was used for the excavation, was sitting at the bottom of the vertical walled excavation without any way of getting out.

But there was a way short of hiring a crane to lift the back-hoe to grade level. Since the excavated material had been deposited on the rim of the excavation, I told the brothers to use some of the material to build an egress ramp for the machine. When the machine reached the grade level they could again remove the ramp with the machine working from the edge of the excavation. There were slapped foreheads and smiles at the suggestion.

About two months or so went by with no problems until I received a call from the client who was noticeably disturbed. "Remember when you told me that I would have a dry basement if we installed the footing drain to go into the lake", he asked. "Of course" I replied. "Well", he said, "how come I have four feet of water in my basement"? "I'll be right there", I said, and left in a hurry.

It had rained for two days over the weekend and I hadn't planned to go to the site until Tuesday. "What could have happened", I thought.

The Clown Brothers were at the site with pumps working to remove what was left of a full basement of water. The Owner arrived shortly after I did and reviewed the pumping work.

The framing had been completed and the roof drains were in place. They terminated into a vertical pipe at grade which was supposed to be connected to the footing drain. The five of us looked at the scene and I asked the question, "Did you connect the leaders into the footing drain"? "Yes" was the answer but Minnie continued, "I didn't think that the footing drain would work on the outside of the footing, so I installed another drain on the inside of the footing to get any of the water which would get under the slab". "What did you connect this drain to"? I asked. "The footing drain on the outside of the footing" was the reply. "You can't do that" was my immediate reply. "You're forcing all the water from the roof to go to the pipe inside the footings and this caused the flood". Another forehead slapping occurred and a look of questioning. "What should we do"? "Break the pipe from the inside drain to the outside drain and fill it with concrete so that no water from the outside drain can get into the inside pipe". Smiles again and out came the sledge hammer to correct the problem.

A week later I got another call from the Owner. "One of my friends came to see the progress of work and asked me why I was having two fireplaces installed side by side" he said. "They had just started on the chimney the previous day and I was there and had checked on the size of the foundation to support the flue, the fireplace and the log holding area. "How could a visitor think that we were putting in two fireplaces", I thought.

Off I went to the site. When I arrived Moe ran up to me and said "I saved your ass, I saved your ass". I went inside and sure enough, there were two, four foot openings in the stone work of the fireplace. "Why are there two four foot openings when one opening is to be for the fireplace and the other was to be a two foot opening for the logs", I said. He said, "I know one is for the fireplace and one is for the logs but I saved your ass, it's a mistake on the drawings. How can you get four foot logs into a two foot wide opening" he demanded. I replied "you turn the logs so they store on end, the stone work is much more than five feet deep". Another forehead slap and immediate directions to revise the stone layout to match the drawings.

In spite of all the questions and forehead slapping, the Clown Brothers did a fine job. The masonry and carpentry were well constructed in a fine workmanship like manner and all concerned were happy at the final result. The house is now in the "must see" list for any potential clients who want to view some of my work.

33. Drunk on the Job:

It is interesting to me that my practice of Architecture has given me a variety of incidences which are not covered by courses in Architectural School. Possibly the one lesson that is most important is not covered in college or apprenticeship. Expect the unexpected and be resourceful to solve the problem created by the unexpected.

I had designed an expensive home for the Owner of a large company. It was the kind of project all Architect's dream of having. This was to be an elegant home for an epicurean couple with no patience for the ordinary. Cost was no object and they wanted luxury. In addition to the fine details of mouldings and trim they wanted the quality of the New York Style mansions of the early twentieth century.

The lady of the house, who was in her early thirties, wanted plaster walls, but walls that didn't crack after curing. I told her that the old plaster homes of the early nineteen hundreds were made with plaster that was set into wooden lathing reinforced with horse hair and that I didn't know if any plastic contractors used this process any more. But I recommended that we use two layers of gypsum board on all the partitions. The first layer would be five-eights of an inch thick screwed to the wood framing. The top layer would be three eighths inch thick and would be glued to the first layer. The result would look like plaster but without the cracking. The process would be more economical in time and money since I didn't know where to find a local lath and plasterer. She accepted my suggestion and I incorporated the double layer of gypsum board in my drawings.

The project went along smoothly. After the framing was complete, she asked if I would contact her when the contractor was installing the double wall finish. She was indeed an elegant lady with a healthy curiosity and a desire to learn. As it turned out, I needed some learning too.

It was time for her visit to see the walls being drywalled and we made a date to meet at the site at noon time. I'm usually early to meetings and arrived about a half hour before time. When I approached the home I heard men laughing and cursing loudly. When I entered the construction, I saw some men wrestling, some lying on the floor and some staggering around aimlessly as if they were drunk. In fact, they were drunk, but not from alcohol. On the floor were large open cans of contact cement. The process required both the first layer of gypsum board to be rolled with contact cement after it was screwed in place. The second layer was to be rolled with cement and then put in place on the prepared first layer. The problem was that the men did not read the warning on the cans of cement which advised them only to work in a well ventilated area. I looked around the room and all the windows were closed and one sniff of the room air gave me the answer.

Fortunately the General Contractor arrived early too, and I told him to get the men out of the house and open the windows. I jumped in my car and drove to the nearest fast food store and ordered hamburgers and black coffee for everybody. When I returned the men were all sitting on the front lawn and all the windows were open. I served each a cup of coffee and a hamburger and announced that lunch was being served by the Owner who was expected shortly.

When she arrived she was happy to see all the smiling faces of the thankful workers and joined me for a tour through the home. The smell was still present but not anywhere near the intoxication level. She was pleased with the progress, and the result of the substituted system. I escorted her out of her home quickly for obvious reasons. She said goodbye and left the site never realizing the panic situation which was present only fifteen minutes earlier. The contractor and I gave a sigh of relief and I was thankful of my new lesson in construction management.

34. Close Call:

I would imagine that every Architect, during his or her career, would have an incident which could have serious consequences. Even though the Architect may not be responsible for the cause of a nasty incident during construction, the foundation less blame continuous irresponsibly.

I had designed a garage and living room addition to a house that was built around 1920. The house was situated on a hill which sloped sharply to the driveway which led to a carriage house in the rear. The carriage house had been removed and the clients wanted to install a new garage in the space between the driveway, in the steep hill, which would connect to the basement of the house. Above the garage was to be a new family room which would also connect to the house at the main floor level.

The Topographic Survey indicated that the driveway, which was twenty-five feet from the house, to be a foot below the basement level. This made it possible for the new garage to have enough headroom for their cars and also allow a downward slope to the garage floor so that any water, which might accumulate in the garage from snow melting off the car, would drain out of the garage to the driveway. The grade would also allow the basement to be about eight inches higher than the garage floor to ensure that no carbon monoxide from the engine exhaust could enter the house.

I had investigated the interior face of the exterior wall of the basement where the garage was to be attached, and found that the wall was a stone wall coated with cement plaster. There were no cracks or any evidence of settlement in the wall. I decided that this wall could remain since we only needed to penetrate the wall with a three foot wide door to get access from the new garage to the existing basement. Since the hill covered the exterior side of the basement wall it couldn't be observed.

The first part of construction was the removal of the hill between the basement and the driveway. This was accomplished without incident during the first week of work which concluded on Friday afternoon. On Saturday morning I decided to take a ride to visit the site. There are no five day weeks for Architects. It was a beautiful sunny day and a ride in the country would be a pleasant distraction from the office.

I parked my car in the driveway next to the excavation and saw the exterior side of the basement wall for the first time. The stones of the wall were easily seen and I wondered why these were not covered by cement plaster as the inside face was. I got out of my car and walked up to the wall. The sun was shining brightly against the wall causing dark contrasting shadows under the individual stones. It was a memorable site indeed.

As I admired the view, I saw what I thought was an ant making a vertical run down the wall.

The strong sunlight and consequent shadow made its run very noticeable. The run was very vertical and quite fast. I was curious about the speed and verticality of what I had observed because ants usually travel in crooked paths and hesitate in their travels. While I was still contemplating what I had just seen, another "ant" did the same thing. This time I followed the shadow down to the bottom of the wall. It wasn't an ant but a grain of sand. On closer inspection I noticed that the mortar joints between the stones consisted of sand particles. I touched the mortar joints between the stone and the sand granules gave way to my fingers and fell to the ground. This should not have happened.

I touched other joints in the masonry and the bulb went off in my brain. Some of the foundation walls in the 1920's were constructed of stones set in wet sand and covered with cement plaster on the interior and with backfilled soil on the exterior. This would account for the short steep hill being so close to the foundation and the cement plaster on the interior. By excavating the soil which formed the hill, and exposing the foundation to the sunlight, the wet sand between the stones was drying and loosening its capability to hold the stones in place. The wall was on its way to crumble, carrying the structure above it to destruction.

I jumped into my car and drove to the Contractor's house, which was about fifteen minutes away. (This was before cell phones). He came to the door when I rang and I said, "Come with me". He followed me in his truck and we viewed the wall together. He saw the problems and agreed with me. The clients were living in the house at the time and they were home. We explained the problems and with the thought that the house in which they lived was about to collapse, it was not difficult for them to agree with the necessity of replacing the wall.

As it turned out, there was no footing under the existing stone wall and a new footing was needed as well. The contractor shored up the existing first floor of the house, removed the stone wall, and built a new footing and foundation for the new garage and house addition. All went well and a Saturday joy ride had saved some difficult moments for my clients and my practice.

35. Turn the Tables on the Greedy:

Sometimes an Architect can make a client very happy without doing very much. This occurred when I was designing a new office for a medical practice. My client had just started his own general medical practice in a building within walking distance from my own office.

His program was simple and typical of a general medical practice as he needed a reception room for ten people, a receptionist station and billing area, four examining rooms, two toilets, a small lab area, a consultation room and secured medical storage area. His newly acquired space was on the first floor of a three story office building.

As he needed interior decorating services, I brought my wife to our first meeting as I knew she was well qualified to design the colors and textures of the new walls and furniture to be incorporated.

At our meeting the Doctor pointed out a coffee table which he had purchased from the Doctor who had just retired causing my client to find a new office and also take on his former patients. This was among many items the retiring doctor sold to my client for about five thousand dollars. The reason my client pointed this out was that the retiring doctor had offered to pay $1,500.00 for the return of the coffee table. My guy was suspicious of the request and asked my wife her opinion on the offer.

It was a hand made table but not something the doctor wanted in his new office as it took up a lot of space and was not in his taste. My wife immediately told him that it was indeed valuable and an offer of $1,500.00 was a lot less than the table was worth. She said that he should contact an auction gallery in New York to get some idea of the value.

A representative from a well known gallery saw the table and offered to auction it off to their clientele in New York City. About a month later the doctor called my wife to offer us a dinner on him. It turned out that the unwanted table sold at auction for $35,000.00 and they were very happy with the result of the auction.

The original doctor must have had the table for as long as he was in practice, which was at least thirty years, the sculptor of the table had died in the interim and the value of the table escalated since there could be no reproductions made any more.

It frightens me to learn that my work may also become more valued after my demise. But I am happy to know that my wife's memory will live forever in the minds of my doctor and his wife.

36. Back to High School:

After spending five years in Architectural School for my Bachelor Degree in Architecture and three years internship at several Architectural firms, and passing the Architectural Licensing Examination, I considered that my education was complete. As a new Architectural Practitioner I was anxious to accumulate clients and render my services to the community.

I was lucky as my first large project was to develop a seventeen acre site to which I referred in "Opening Office", mentioned earlier.

My reputation grew and more projects came my way. Since I chose not to specialize in any particular type of building, such as, religious, educational, etc., I was ready to do anything that came my way. Consequently I accepted a commission to Design a Precious Metals Refining and Plating Plant.

The project was a challenge because the site had poor soil quality and I needed to design the footings resting on thirty foot long wooden piles driven into the soil. This was my first project with piles. My college structural courses came back to me and with the help of my Structural Consultant I had no problem with the Pile Design.

But the Owner raised another problem. Their process of metal plating required large vessels of hydrochloric acid into which the metals were placed during the plating process. The vapors given off by these vessels of acid were very corrosive. The Owner wanted assurance that any steel structure over the plating room would be protected against the air borne fumes.

Since the smallest dimension of the plating room was thirty feet he felt that a steel frame would be the most economical structural system to provide a column free space. But the steel had to be covered with a chlorinated rubber paint which would seal off the vapors and keep the steel from corroding. But wait, I had an idea. I remembered my Chemistry Class from High School in which we discussed hydrochloric acid being stored in wooden vats. I went to the cellar of my house and dusted off my High School Chemistry text book. (I never discarded any book that I ever possessed). I dusted it off and found the Section on HCL. My thought was confirmed.

The next day I proposed that we span the Plating Room with laminated wood beams and wood decking concealing all the metal connections. I knew they made such hardware to keep the steel from weathering and this application would apply here. My client agreed and the material of the design was set. We ended up with a beautiful plating room of long span laminated wood beams about sixteen feet apart with laminate tongue and groove decking forming the ceiling and roof structure. In the end the room could have been a Family Room in a palatial house. All were pleased with the result.

37. THE BIBLE TELLS US SO:

I was in charge of the Construction Administration of a large Catholic Church in Southern New Jersey. The Church complex consisted of a Sanctuary, School, Library, Gymnasium and Rectory.

Ed Savior was President of the General Construction Company which was awarded the construction contract after the competitive bidding. In addition to being a licensed professional engineer he was also a certified pilot. He flew both fixed wing and rotary wing air craft.

At the beginning of the construction he requested permission to land his helicopter on the construction site. I had no objections and neither did the Priest in charge.

At the outset of the construction the Priest had some questions regarding the sequence and timing of the construction as the existing building was being sold and the potential buyer was concerned about a closing date if the sale was consummated.

The Priest called me to arrange an urgent meeting with the contractor to determine when the closing date could be confirmed. I arranged for a meeting at the site at 9:00 a.m. of the following morning.

I met the Priest at 8:50 a.m. and saw a nervous soul pacing the bare spot of earth where the topsoil had been removed the previous day. "I need to know the timing" he said, "I don't want to have the deal lost because of timing". "Where is Ed, he asked, I need help on this".

And then the memorable moment came and it makes me smile every time I recall it. In the distance I heard a helicopter which was coming directly at us. I looked at the Priest and pointed at the helicopter and said "look into the hills from whence cometh your help, the savior arrives".

It was Ed Savior and he landed about fifty feet from us. The Priest was stunned and I was still smiling. I don't remember the conversation but the meeting didn't last long and the Priest left satisfied. Ed took off shortly thereafter and I waved goodbye as he turned his ship 180° at ten feet altitude and flew away. I knew then that I would remember this meeting forever.

38. THE COVER:

The cover of this book best represents the frustration of Architectural Practice, the desire to satisfy the Client, and the Research and Creativity, all of which makes the Practice of Architecture a totally involved and rewarding way of life.

The project was to design a manufacturing facility as an addition to an old industrial building which would be functional to the process of making folding cartons, an advertisement to the public and quick and economical to build.

The interior of the building had to accommodate large lithograph machines which stamped out large cardboard sheets containing many reproductions of the folding boxes in which were placed over-the-counter medications. The machines were about fifty feet long and needed additional footings.

Once the layout of the machines was determined, it was relatively easy to design a column grid to accommodate the required spacing.

I decided early on that to shorten the construction time and to accommodate the required height of the interior space the building should be clad in pre-cast concrete panels. These could be eight to twelve feet wide, six or eight inches thick and up to twenty-four feet high.

The problem arose as to the design of the exterior. Several of my schemes were rejected by the Owner as looking too much like other industrial buildings in the area. Even the "in-house artist" employed by the Owner couldn't come up with a design to incorporate the solution to the building program and the Owner's desire to have an advertisement of his building.

At one memorable meeting with the Owner I said out of frustration. "You're in the folding carton business, why don't we make the building like a folding carton"? "I love the idea", he said, and the rest is history.

Every client I have had since the building was completed knew of and had seen this building. It has been a great selling point for me and my practice. I ask each client, "who else but a nut could design something like that and they love it". They tell me it indicates my commitment to my clients and my ability to go beyond normal construction methods to satisfy an unusual situation.

39. What's Next?

I don't intend to retire as long as I can hold a pencil and speak intelligently. I hope my book of confessions will touch the hearts and minds of other Architects in whatever stage of practice they are involved and spread the word to the rest of the Non-Architects that Architecture as a Profession is fun and enlightening and can be enjoyed by all. The key is, as it must be in all professions, to listen with an open mind, remember your education, seek out a solution however long it takes, and enjoy the comments of a happy client. Make the world a better place for one client and you make the world a better place for all of us.

Printed in the United States
201962BV00001B/133-303/P